Dear Readers,

When Elijah McCoy was a little boy, his parents knew the importance of a good education. They showed Elijah the importance of working very hard.

When Elijah grew up, he made an invention that made life better for everyone. No one else could make a copy as good as his original. His invention made him famous and wealthy.

Whenever you begin a project of any kind, give it your all. Do the best possible job, just like Elijah McCoy.

Your friend,

Garnet Jackson

Elijah McCoy | Inventor

Written by Garnet Nelson Jackson
Illustrated by Gary Thomas

 MODERN CURRICULUM PRESS

Program Reviewers

Maureen Besst, Teacher
　　Orange County Public Schools
　　Orlando, Florida

Carol Brown, Director of Reading
　　Freeport Schools
　　Freeport, New York

Kanani Choy, Principal
　　Clarendon Alternative School
　　San Francisco, California

Barbara Jackson-Nash, Deputy Director
　　Banneker-Douglass Museum
　　Annapolis, Maryland

Minesa Taylor, Teacher
　　Mayfair Elementary School
　　East Cleveland, Ohio

MODERN CURRICULUM PRESS

13900 Prospect Road, Cleveland, Ohio 44136

A Paramount Communications Company

Copyright © 1993 Modern Curriculum Press, Inc.

Library of Congress Catalog Card Number: 92-28797
ISBN 0-8136-5230-8 (Reinforced Binding)　　ISBN 0-8136-5703-2 (Paperback)

10 9 8 7 6 5 4 3　　　　　　97 96 95 94 93

Text Printed on Recycled Paper

Swish Swissh Swisssh Swisssssh!
The train wheels came to a halt.
It was oiling time again.

A little over 100 years ago, trains did not move as fast as they do today.

A train would run a while before the engine slowed to a stop. Then workers would have to oil every moving part before the train could start again.

It would take days and days, sometimes weeks, before cargo was delivered. Sometimes goods would spoil or rot on the way.

There lived in a little Canadian town called Colchester, Ontario, a small boy named Elijah McCoy. Like most children, he liked trains. He loved watching the trains near his home and listening to the *swish swish* sounds of the big wheels.

But he did not know how hard it was to keep those big wheels turning. He did not know that, if they were not stopped and oiled many times, the wheels would be unable to move.

Elijah was the McCoys' greatest joy. His parents, Mildred and George, had been runaway slaves from Kentucky who fled the United States to Canada.

They took great pride in their young son. George worked many long hours to make sure Elijah had a good education.

7

Some time later the family moved to Ypsilanti, Michigan. Elijah spent much of his spare time trying to design and improve machines.

Before he finished school, he left for Scotland. There Elijah studied to become a mechanical engineer.

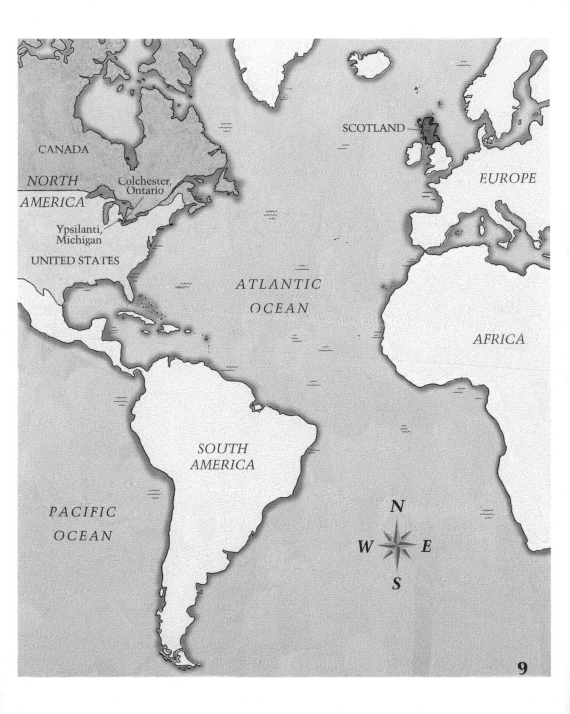

CANADA

NORTH
AMERICA

Colchester,
Ontario

Ypsilanti,
Michigan

UNITED STATES

SCOTLAND

EUROPE

ATLANTIC
OCEAN

AFRICA

PACIFIC
OCEAN

SOUTH
AMERICA

N

W   E

S

9

Elijah learned to be a great engineer. Then he returned to the United States in search of a job.

But because of his color, Elijah could not find a job as an engineer. So he settled for a job as an oiler for trains. This was quite a lowly job for the fine engineer he was.

As Elijah oiled the wheels, he
remembered the *swish swish*
sounds of the wheels he loved as
a boy.

Now he knew how hard it was to
keep them moving, and how
long it took a train to get from
place to place.

Elijah thought, "There must be some way that a train can be oiled while moving."

That way it would never have to
stop. And the wheels would continue
to go *swish swish*.

After much thinking, in 1872 Elijah McCoy made a new part for trains. This part dripped oil onto the moving wheels and the engine while the train was rolling along the tracks. Elijah called his new part a *lubricator.*

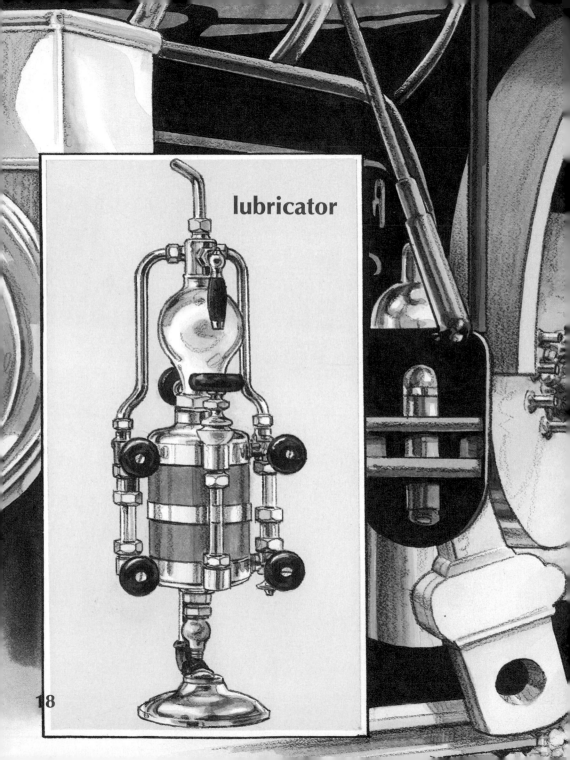

lubricator

News about the lubricator
spread. Railroad people
everywhere were happy.
Trains no longer had to stop
to be oiled.

Elijah invented lubricators for other machines, too. People in businesses all over the world were buying Elijah McCoy's lubricators.

Since everyone wanted to buy lubricators, other people tried to make and sell them. But theirs just did not work as well as Elijah's.

Merchants wanted to make sure they were not getting a copy. So when they went to buy a lubricator, they always asked for "the real McCoy."

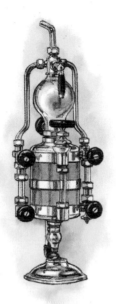

Elijah became famous and wealthy as one of the greatest mechanical engineers of his time.

And from that day, our world has never been the same. McCoy's ideas are still used in lubricators for cars, trains, planes, and many other machines. And the saying "the real McCoy" is still used to describe "the very best."

Glossary

engineer (en jə nir´) 1. A person who runs an engine, such as a railroad locomotive. 2. A person who plans and builds engines and other machines, roads, bridges, and buildings.

lubricator (loo´ bri kāt ər) Something that adds oil or other material to a thing to make it smooth

machine (mə shēn´) Anything that is made of one or more parts, often moving parts, to do work

mechanical engineer (mə kan´ i k′l en jə nir´) An engineer who plans and builds new machines or makes machines run better

merchant (mʉr´ chənt) A person, such as a store owner, who makes a living by buying and selling

slave (slāv) A person who is owned by someone else, and must do whatever the owner wants

About the Author

Garnet Jackson is an elementary teacher in Flint, Michigan, with a deep concern for developing a positive self-image in young African American students. After an unsuccessful search for materials about famous African Americans written on the level of early readers, Ms. Jackson filled the gap by producing a series of biographies herself. In addition to being a teacher, Ms. Jackson is a poet and a newspaper columnist. She has one son, Damon. She dedicates this book to the memory of her dear mother, Carrie Sherman.

About the Illustrator

Gary Thomas, a native of Ohio, has worked as a commercial illustrator for over thirty years. His distinctive, photo-realistic style can be seen in many illustrations in the U.S. Olympic, Pro Football, and Bowling Halls of Fame. In *Elijah McCoy*, Thomas combines watercolor and charcoal to capture the aura of trains of the past with a precise technical sensitivity.